THE SWING IN THE MIDDLE OF CHAOS

Sylva Fischerová was born in 1963 in Prague. She grew up in the Moravian town of Olomouc as a daughter of non-Marxist philosopher whose works were banished under communist rule. She returned to Prague to study philosophy and physics, and later Greek and Latin, at Charles University where she now teaches ancient Greek literature and philosophy. She has published six volumes of poems in Czech, and her poetry has been translated and published in numerous languages. She recently began to write prose, and a book of her stories, *Miracle*, as well as a book for children, appeared in 2005.

She has published two selections of her poetry in English, both with Bloodaxe Books, *The Tremor of Racehorses*, translated by Ian & Jarmila Milner (1990), and *The Swing in the Middle of Chaos: Selected Poems*, translated by Sylva Fischerová with Stuart Friebert (2010).

SYLVA FISCHEROVÁ

THE
SWING
IN THE MIDDLE OF
CHAOS

SELECTED POEMS

TRANSLATED BY
SYLVA FISCHEROVÁ
& STUART FRIEBERT

BLOODAXE BOOKS

First published 2010 by
Bloodaxe Books Ltd,
Highgreen,
Tarset,
Northumberland NE48 1RP.

www.bloodaxebooks.com
For further information about Bloodaxe titles
please visit our website or write to
the above address for a catalogue.

Supported by
**ARTS COUNCIL
ENGLAND**

Cover design: Neil Astley & Pamela Robertson-Pearce.

Printed in Great Britain by
Bell & Bain Limited, Glasgow, Scotland.

ACKNOWLEDGEMENTS

This selection is drawn from the following Czech collections: *Velká zrcadla* (1990), *V podsvětním městě* (1994), *Šance* (1999), *Krvavý koleno* (2005) and *Anděl na okně* (2007). Thanks to the editors of the following journals, in which some of these translations have appeared, sometimes in slightly different form: *Field, Great River Review, Hayden's Ferry Review, The Literary Review, Pleiades, The Round Table* and *Turnrow*. A few of the translations intentionally differ from the Czech originals. Thanks to Justin Quinn and Andrew Jan Hauner for valuable suggestions. This translation has been subsidised by the Ministry of Culture of the Czech Republic.

CONTENTS

I

Butterfly Museum

Inventing metaphors
is my best art,
wrapping up the world with words
for not to fall.
Everything raises a claim on everything:
Siberia on Sahara,
the yellow fields of rape
shine in the middle of the sea,
golden Buddhas
float on thoughts as
on flying carpets,
high above the palisades of scholastics,
above the stake where Master Hus is broiled.
It stitches the world together, so that it looks
like patched trousers.
There's a draught from below.
The dead smile their cracked smiles.
They know but
they won't tell.

I'm a telescope crossed with a kaleidoscope,
but used contrarily
to watch magnetised puppets
rising up and sitting down
under heaven's power plant,
while the tape recorder repeats:
      *Gimme your cause
      like the prophet Jeremiah!*
The world below
is tinkered together by words
for not to fly:
bound, distinct, separated, named,
museum of night and day butterflies,
beautiful even in vitrines.
The night ones are greater.
The living are better.

Visitors prepare legends,
each in his own dialect
of proper names and memories.

Who has no language,
speaks in parables.

Hell, The Soul, Banners

So, today love's just
            infidelity.
So, all of us who thought
    we can do what we want
    we needn't we can't just want
    we can want what we want

all of us will meet in Hell
under extremely gruesome punishments
    in the midst of alien children, and find
                your own
        in the midst of alien women, and find
                yourself
        in the midst of fathers and mothers
            and all of them yours
        amid gods and grain and sperm
        within the soul and free will
            where there's nothing
            just winds fluttering
                like banners.

The Worm

Far away in the dark nothingness there's a worm saying
God exists
and deep in God there's a worm that doesn't
want Him
but nobody knows if it's the same worm, nobody wants
to undergo the journey, report the journey
nobody knows, nobody can
he wouldn't come back
doesn't know where to go, right or left? Or climb up a high tower,
look over the sky, choose his own spot
and jump down
or set forth into the wedding veil
shinny up the forehead of an idea, not that original,
that important
and begin again on the first page of the primer:
'Breathe your body,
drink up your blood,
hear your ears,
force your eyes to watch
your own purgatory:
Kiss your soul, my dear,
kiss your soul.'

Like Everybody

Like everybody, I'm just
a demon preparing her own
destruction:
building a house
bricked up with plans, memories and wind,
moving her hands
on the memories
as on a chessboard
while the board moves back
like the eyes of the chess players.

The wind will blow all this away,
even the thoughts you've wrapped yourself in
like flesh on your frame.
You'll remain alone, just you,
a clod of similes
with an old alibi
that the Last Judgment
won't take place till tomorrow.

I'M

The candle's burning
and there's nothing to say   alone and sad
    a man sits facing the flame
What will happen? he asks, but doesn't know
He lists all his I-don't-understands
As if knowing
    could save him
Knowing that can drown
    even a full-grown rat!
Plunge it into the Eternal Fire,
the fire of pride, which will burn up the world,
            that launching crematorium
            embedded in me, myself & I:
            which you water like a flower, say
                Alpine asters...
– But I means liberty! Liberty punched
into a mould,
I'M is a mud pie!
A mould for the beginning of all crimes,
I, Cain listening to the Lord:
            'Am I not ready to accept you too,
            if you do well?'
and then he goes to kill
                Abel
because he must
    because Abel doesn't understand why he isn't
                Cain
I'M
goaded by Death like a gadfly –
I'M definite, irreplaceable, perfect
like everyone else.

Land of Mud
(Warsaw-Leningrad Express)

And it wasn't till the middle of the night we saw
smoke over the locomotive
when all those villages
and their mud for straw, straw for shoes
                              disappeared
The child ate too many bullets from the war
and is so heavy
it'll fall in a while
into the plain full of Lenins and Christs
but no hill
so mad-prophet children
will be born here again
from the mud
and their fathers will wait
until the child finds
an old book in the attic
and it'll begin all over again
in the land of mud
And women stood along the tracks
thinking the locomotive was going to the place
where the reason is
why they give birth
to prophetic children
of mud
and the women waved scarves of mud
at the straw train
in the land of mud

The Moons of Things

After the gods,
just the chunks of bread
          as forgotten libations,
and silence.
Time disappeared under the eyelids,
its sea spuming
after the moons of things –
in the evening, something falls into the well,
we say – Life gets easier and easier,
     a feather.

Soldier in the Blue Uniform of Forgiving

Every day
   from the crack of dawn
   the gods forgive our bad deeds,
every day the fabric of the Law
   rips, you try to mend it but
         the borders shift,
   you stick your hands up,
   try to touch
   the edge of the heavens, blue colour
      of forgiving,
   catch the beauty.
Every day you weave a part
   of the Law's fabric,
not knowing where you'll weave tomorrow,
   you're just a soldier – a soldier
   in the blue uniform of forgiving.

Lazarus, White Holly Berries

They're always three:
        one laughs,
        the second cries,
        and the third is silent,
    kneels lies walks
    and those standing
    pray over Lazarus.

They're always three, three ladies
saying Yes, yes,
    it's really
      a very nice house
      with a holly bower.
Holly
is for Lazarus:
    it's green and pricks
    and its white berries
    are all the next lives,
        Lazarus,
        look carefully.

Lazarus looks and thinks it's the
        Beginning, Middle, and End,
        but he wants Paradise.
    You think there's
    Paradise, Lazarus? Lazarus, get up and walk
                    on the endless
                    holly berries,
    choose once,
    twice,
    a third time. Three Lazaruses on
        the nine-fold
        edge of holly.

This Century Blossoms Black and Green

We're all just an image of an era,
solution to its equation.
And in the era's frame, again that
masquerade of death, that doll with wooden legs
who blindly, smoothly like a dancer,
leads us
towards a place where leaves don't fall,
there's no spring, summer, autumn or winter –
as in this province of the world, history, spirit,
where the equation isn't solved, but everything's
its solution, ready in advance,
because arithmetic's been invented by someone,
who wanted to chase after false results!
    And you, you thought that memory's
the tree of life, you scrambled against time,
wanted to break through, where
presence
grows like a graft from eternity.
You wanted to see the right hawthorn.
This century
    blossoms black and green.
In the evening
the dark mists of technology and alcohol,
of Treblinka and pollen
                  from rustic apple trees,
rise from it...
Hope like a billiard ball
wobbles in the air.
And parents have sent their boy over the hill
to see a prophet on the white throne,
who won't tell him why he was born.
He'll say
he doesn't know...
Dear mourners will eat
    the stag with cranberries,
their mouths greasy,

missing the letters
on their foreheads
like the Prague Golem,
God took them away,
because He got angry with them.

Encased in Laurels

That longing to touch yourself
   in the striped dress on the merry-go-round,
an appetite for turning time back
   gazing into its eyes
      at the colour of its hair
      its wind
is just a desire to reach into the bloody flank
   of the resurrected Christ
   grasp grace
      palpable as sinew
   your own immortality
   in Paradise with paramours, angels and roasted pigeons
   but encased in laurels and the imperishable
      memory of descendants.

Near the Bottom

But behind the end, near the bottom,
a longing to be like everyone else:
walking around your house
as if around the mist,
planting a tree,
and misunderstanding the prophets.
I also wanted
to eat oysters with lemon
somewhere in Montmartre,
I also wanted peace and money,
and the bright colours of stones underwater.
Those bright colours underwater!

On the Chances

How about it?
How about this house
on the edge of the forest?
People call the place 'On the Chances'
and it's a chance for you and me –
after all those hospital nights
                    of prayers,
all those days devoured by the hospital TV
irrevocably, without any rest,
                    like a herring.
Chances not to walk around
            thoughts and words
to open heart and body
unconditionally, forever,
    as if putting your head
    on the chopping block,
and to see the heavens' phenomena
set on children's foreheads:
an angel hangs on every strand of hair,
and like on the French horn
plays on joy.
The sky imitates
        their smiles...
But us! If we could understand
just one thing absolutely –
if we could grasp
            a daisy!
But we breathe ignorance like air,
eat it like manna,
our eyes veiled, wandering the world
with a foolish command
NOT TO KILL, NOT TO DESTROY
even the petal of a jasmine –
where the amputated limbs salute us
    from the greasy Gulag
    the fridge of the well-off.

And the golden light of the Milky Way,
soothed by angels' feet,
falls over it all.
If we could understand just one thing
                    absolutely,
the world would be lost.

Warm Evening in May

And under the cloudy sky
the toothy gable of the roof
    looking like a backdrop
of the gingerbread cottage,
the moon a floodlight,
and you're the bourgeoise gazing at it!

Where have the children run off to?
And will they, as we did,
want to turn adult just like that,
drink coffee, smoke in the morning,
and sleep in bus stations,
living in a world encased in books
    so it won't fall down
while it stands on
the nights children sleep
on the castle built up
by their breath.

Will they make
    the same mistakes?
Look for meaning
among weasels' heads crackling,
where meteors whiz through the universe,
in the middle of which
there's a white garden table,
    white chairs,
and our men, our women
throw leg over leg, sitting
there drinking their coffee.
They open their mouths but
    nothing's heard.
Why did they disappear so far?

Children have drawn them and now
they're buying leaves, selling sand,
performing: the left hand
gives money to the right,
    the price of a plantain doll,
of a leg of bugbear who loves them!
As everyone does...

Children will lead the bourgeois
right up to Heaven's Gate.

And Even When Looking for Names

As when striking a horseshoe
and the anvil, the floor, the whole house
                         begin to vibrate,
and beyond the hill a man turns back,
What? What's this? he says.
And even when looking for names
the trees respond, following
the edge of the knife –
the man hears them
in the ring of the horseshoe,
and gropes for the heart of things,
touches a little hollow of dark water
as if flown out of the quartz.
Names! There, inside,
that's where the crystal is,
and a little girl's pounding away
at the plaster with her hammer,
because the wall can't fall,
the words of translation
drop into the cauldron of the epoch,
dust, weeds, and teeth,
let Life end other than it began,
let the graves not reach beyond
the hanging gardens.

In the Underworld City

Brother, where have you found yourself?
In the underworld city, and there were houses there,
and darkness,
and a man who led me didn't speak,
just pointed into the dark.
People were standing there, speaking but
not a word was heard.
I asked him: Who's the woman with swollen cheeks,
turning her face away from you and me?
I don't know, he said, even you don't want to know.
But I wanted to know.
And they told me people will do anything for money
in the city built on streets of gold,
and that I'll hear only what I want to, even if I don't want to.
Brother, they told me, the woman,
for the amusement of the rich,
breeds little rodents in her ear.

The Underworld City

...and as if you were without hands, only
the winds skid you to the Gate of Grief.
They're drinking there. In the underworld city
even the animals booze, tigers drink brandy
and revile history. What liberty,
when time is a fence
and man something
in the gutter full of chuckholes,
something leading his fathers
through the gutter till the edge of time,
and they're dying in the middle of the journey

From the procession of principles
boredom drops like bonbons,
blood-red like beets.
And Diabolos in the ear whispers
this city's an advertisement,
a coulisse built for a movie
nobody will understand –

Break off that resigned note; the slowness of
the dough that bore the germ
of a thought
and now it's drowning in the inertial tremble of jelly;
that anonymity of ham actors gaping
in the grey morning at the carpet of wooden cubes,
there's Emanuel playing, the saviour of the world,
compound
of the fibres of cooked beef.
The world is a placenta, will we find
the child?

II

In the Bloody Dream of Words

You can't take it back now.
Everything straightens and doesn't
cast a shadow
so that a man fades away,
a man, shadow of a shadow,
shadow in the dream,
a dream of a shadow –

Time funnels, growing like a pyramid.
The road to it is bordered by flowers.
Singers sing
        well-known stories
        with unknown endings.
A meat dish is served. What's
                    above?
A tapered man,
chokered by his choices, gasping,
rises up through the chamber of gifts and lies
and not slept-out mornings,
                    of love.
All his selves are falling down.
He throws them at the others. What is
above? What is
down? He listens to
his story, to an arc of breath
cast to the flowers,
        to the shadow of a dream of flowers.
Will he recognise his story
        in the bloody dream of words?

All Their Life

All their life
they lived in a place
where they conceived a child
all their life
they walked around the place
where God left him
the Ark of the Covenant
which they weren't able to read
        just to sign.

The White Bones of the World

This history's yours.
You repeat every mistake of mankind.
You tried to take
             God's tomb.
You sailed to the New World,
    brought back natives, red pepper
                          and coffee.
You waved a flag like
a statue of the Revolution.
You let the children die of the plague.
And then you sat in the corner
             and cried.

That's the West:
    bone on bone
    stone on stone
    a castle a knight
    captures but then
    loses at dice,
    comes to camp, drinks soup with the monks
    cooked from the white bones of the world...
    And for dessert, wine and fruit,
    which is sad
        as a gate of the West
    and tastes like liquor from Armenian apples,
    all those shining gold apples of the East
    hurrying to the funeral of Greece,
    to the cauldron of Chaironeia.

The Blind

There's nothing for Lie
                    to gain
                but itself
how you walk among its houses in ruins
its forests of words and pauses

Lie floats on trembling sands
like a snake eating its own tail
till it finds itself back at the beginning

There's a chessboard with
the pieces refigured:
the king's a bishop,
the queen a rook,
the knight's on foot
So Lie reaches under the table
pulls out a Man, a Woman,
and puts them before the Father of Lie
on a high throne
Behind him
stands Treachery:
a new piece
    with a red jaw
The throne's built of
the eyes of those he deluded
and blind men and women
walk the world
one from another, to another,
the chessboard's
interwoven
with fine threads of cries
the blind hold onto
so they can
        move on

The World Is Full of Flowers

The heart is deceitful above all things,
and desperately wicked: who can know it?'
JEREMIAH

And why won't evil win?
Why it looks like
        the things you loved?

It's love that confounds things,
clothes new bodies, new masques,
it's blood and treachery
exchanging itself for itself,
and this is a market, with overgrown swede turnips,
wooden carts, sword-lilies,
and wonderful figurines of women,
oh there's everything!
And so love changes till it's exchanged,
and the heart cries, but in the end
sees it's the most powerful,
because the most deceitful...

And this is a likeness:
like-man, like-woman,
in a like-world
of exchanged hearts,
red sword-lilies
cleaved into the heart.
The killers calmly walk the streets,
left the flowers in the wound,
and return to market for new ones,
their slain move towards them,
and beside them and with them
the world is full of flowers.

Days When I Don't Know How to Live

There are days when I don't know
             how to live,
don't know why a woman
moves opposite me,
one nose,
two eyes,
puts leg before leg
on the pavement
of square grey tiles, why
squares,
on the square a man stands, one nose,
two eyes, whites vitreous,
both in coloured scraps,
concealing what connects
                them,
how they can go, stand
             in a round morning
the phones are ringing
someone calling someone
everybody everyone
blond, dark, thin
all in the infinity of self
how can they fit on?
It's close here
the glass desk of air
   cracks
and blood drips on the floor of the tram
they start to move
instructed to save life,
vitreous eyes,
scrap of self,
and scrap of you,
square
circle

God
sitting in the middle
playing hide-and-seek
seven days a week

Sudden Feeling

A sudden feeling, that this vision of the world as an unclear, cruelly
        disconnected –
where is, but with violence, some sense implanted for us to survive –
is original and true. The world endowed with sense and meaning –
rich in charms, combed women, sightseeing towers,
in the palette of lipstick shades, as well as in Kantian dichotomies –
is but a superstructure, a stubborn, cosmetic effort to make beauty
        from the monster,
it's the supreme act of a painter who, from disconnected lines,
makes a mother bend to the child, a Madonna whose dead son
is to save the world ground to forcemeat, too...

A Beach in Nabeul, Africa

The land sent its clouds over the sea
up to Rome,
let Caesar saddle them
the way Scipio and Cato saddled the Puns.
Here. Names from textbooks, faces
from steles: Roman coiffures, Etrurian smiles.
And all along, memorise, memorise,
what in fact happened otherwise.
History is a bad memory of mankind.
Bad memory of teacher –
delusion of distance, a mask
of fantasy, my mask: it's me who writes
a false history of me.
And of you.
But they'll take it literally,
with a pomp of harangues,
gallons of saliva
flow from speakers' mouths
into the beer pipes.
Here's to!
To what? To Christ and Antichrist,
but, first of all, to us!

Seaweed on the beach
looks like chocolate fettuccine
sent from over the sea.
Thanks, Julius Gaius!
A boy moulds a Medusa's head
from it.
It's alive. Her hair
will sting you,
her look
change you into an abyss.

Road to Nowhere

We were silent in the trams
passing by yards fenced in grooved metal
our heads a seething pharmacy
    of bad intentions
    and good ideas
on the road to nowhere.
There was the Temple of Technology
made of newspapers,
its windows millboard,
the tower of matches,
and an altar of Industry
all alcohols
    poured down from –
The Angels of Odd floated in the air,
drinking vodka,
biting into the incense of revolution.
It smelled
like the end of the holiday.
Is this a man? Is this a God?

But still, poetry lived there,
shedding from the pale intestines of the city.
We ran after her,
a pack of desperates and expectants –

scraping through the ravine
    of an umbel time, –
behind the words,
where you're burned out, bathed,
    forever branded,
and from the brand all questions
        rise!

Who Makes History

Who has grief and who has sorrow?
Who has a thousand years of woe?

– Impossible to sleep
with the roaring crowds of the elected
They pound on the gate
The glass of air shatters
Seconds pour out
and History phosphoresces
            in the flash of battles
when time's just stuffing
      for the funeral guilds
How eagerly the brothers drink
from their immense steins!
And heads empty, a gutted field
            of lost battles

History phosphoresces, through the loopholes
                  you can see
statues of mustard, statues of tears
pounding on the gate,
crying: *History's made by evil people!*
crunching their lunch
Fate's a lunch
      a brunch
Fate's overcrunched!

Who makes history?
  Human inconsistency makes history
  Time makes history
            see how it spits
            its time-killing liquors
            into throats knotted
                  in the clouds of self
                  like footnotes

notes under the foot
of the universe,
and of free will,
meaning guilt,
mine as well as yours!

A White Ball of Ephedrin

The world is bittersweet.
I have it on my tongue.
Somebody supplies
my body with pain.
Over the ball of the world,
there are people and cosmic worms –
people composed
of doctor visits and wisecracks
dropping from them
like buttons from a mountain goat.
Everybody's an author of his fate!
Dearie, I can't stand it anymore.
So let it go! I'll cry to the ceiling,
to rid us all of it!
The cosmic worms
swarm furiously,
still better than wisecracks,
that mud of common sense,
slimy gossip over coffee and tea,
over everything that flows
and takes away
filtered mornings, aborted
dialogues, but I wanted
to say to you –
wait, it's on my tongue,
like world,
world is wisecrack!
– World as monstrance,
says the priest, but world
packed in cellophane,
a birthday gift.
I have to wait
till somebody gives it to me,
nicely inscribed,
Till death us do part.

The Pharaoh's Daughter

'I'm Catholic,' said the prostitute, put on her hat
                and kept walking
'I believe in God,' he said and went off
                to his mistress
'We're leprous,' said Charles and he was right,
sure we're leprous, they say the pharaoh's daughter
stepped naked into the Nile because she was leprous,
in the river a basket floated with a tiny Moses,
she reached for it and was healed just like that,
her skin like alabaster they
could make chests, vials and memorial candles from,
which we give to the wedding guests to remember, not to forget.

Childhood's God

There's a meadow of old white
                    dandelions,
no human force can blow them out
to total death.
Monotonous blocks of dorms are there,
            doors next to doors,
            a finky porter,
            red and yellow tiles:
devouring the beginning, no end in sight.
When I turn back, my dead father's
lying on the meadow of old dandelions,
a monstrous body of childhood upon him:
        Yes, this was a mother,
        there's an aged sister,
        and the wind in the air, blowing
        white puffs on the corpse – that's me
        in the dotted dress
        with a child's purse
        stepping on the hand, the leg,
        the shoulder.
It's my cemetery.
I go there often
without flowers, which raise themselves
with horrible speed, it's their job,
growing old, cranky, and white.
They're waiting for the wind from the god of childhood.
But now, the god of childhood's only me.

Thirty-fifth Birthday

Years washed ashore like stones in a creek...
My thirty-five years that fought among themselves
and then lay down,
indicators pointing to the end,
but nothing for descendants, nothing
for pilgrims.
I'm walking along the river
      among guffawing gulls,
there's never been such brightness
at the outset of November,
the swans are floating here and away
and my heart's a cloister bell
      in the hour between two masses –

Time, beyond measure, ever artful,
has revolved in itself, taken away places,
chosen and hidden deep in the city's rushes,
the stone primer, and milk coffee
                  in the morning bars
when all the wall inscriptions
spoke of you...
Thirty-five years! And time pranced like a horse,
red and cruel,
through the word outloved as night –
bathed in the creek water of the universe...
And I, the queen of vanity, flowed under the side
      flung out from the angels' dreambook
      as if under sail
right here to this spot, the courtyard with six sundials
but armed with a sword raised
      against nostalgia,
that false coat of eternity, a colouring book of impression.
I saw the gray side of the truth
that never wins.
The winner is the white which flows around
      the brackens of the heart...

The gaggle of bright swans fights with the gulls.
My years like the stones washed ashore,
stopping for a moment
        embodied with fate and name
in the creek water
murmuring to the sides:
        A beast has the life of a beast,
        a mayfly the life of a mayfly
        but we are
        made to return and not to find,
        to go ahead
                and slum on the forehead of the wind,
        hear the white moss
                talking to the heather.
        Hear, as a tree
                hears its leaves…
I'm going through the upright gate of my birthday
harnessed to the question
and under the sword of the secret
and my heart's the bell of a cloister
        in the hour between two masses

Who Eats the Fruit of the Tongue?

Was there ever a possibility
of giving into dolts?
Of being resigned to the world, and language,
which live together
in a dark community,
because they must, not must, but want to –
'Life and Death are in the power of the tongue
and those who love it will eat
its fruit.'
– But I know the sweet smell
of the fruit of Death, all day long I used
to go through its gardens,
full of pre-death masks, nobody knew
his own face, enveloped by the years
and bygone odours, poured the words into bird feeders,
had posters and flags
to hail the history that ground him down
to sausage, salted him over like smoked meat.
And that was
the sweet smell of the fruit of Death...
Who eats the fruit of the tongue?
What illuminates the shadow to its bone?
Why don't we know the shape of feelings?
Only know, bending over a sleeping child,
that there's nothing more, that evil
won't win... although it doesn't know it...
and even if it won, you couldn't
accept it, never!
You couldn't accept Never,
ruffling in the lacquered black Universe.

The Language of the Fountains

I was holding a mirror in my hands for you,
and the ends of your shaved beard
floated in the soapy water,
little, everyday deaths.
The epochs stuck together like veneer to wood,
tight and precise, with a breath between
by which a monster changes
   into a genius,
and the cafeteria's windows into mirrors,
in front of which the dumb goblins learn to speak,
to score
   a defeat.
A defeat of a nation.
And of all dead languages.
The era of quotation marks has begun:
a double mockery at the ideas
   inflated inside them.

But the salt statues still stand by the Dead Sea,
there's still Jerusalem, Athens, Rome,
still someone lives in Prague speaking Yiddish –
and memory, sister to self, sister of sin,
and guide to the saved
   leads us back
   to our own destruction.
Here the cafeteria's a church for smokers!
Defeat's a beer.
Cowardice
   a bridge into time,
and whoever knows a thing about time
will tell of even a God –
will answer God,
   that hole inside him
   the coloured nooses of history
   fall from.

And the rich and powerful fit nice and tight...
Who will tell of the dead children
    on the trembling sands of history?
Who will see – will hear
    the language of the fountains, sweet, predictable
    as a throw of dice?
Who will speak of all the dead children
    on the trembling sands of history...

Death

At first she's geometrical,
crystalline like doom,
and then numerous visits
of shadows in the silent house –
Then she comes naked, a mourning band on her hand
on the autopsy table;
and we start to draw fruits,
quietly pulling out pastels,
saying:
>Sense, there must be
>a sense,
>mythical snake
>will embrace world again.
And then it'll be safe.
Like a cop –
safeguarding houses and gardens,
where I also pertain, and there's a garden plot
with my sinful name,
so I have a chance and can move out
in it, from it,
I, a tree with roots –
solidifying the way to the supermarket,
where I'll find a cart.
Death – death! Stifle death,
eat her like intestines, stomp on her,
break her, burn her!
And then let her be, stand her
in the corner.
What's the grass torn out
by the mad Hölderlin?
What's the thing
that comes in through windows
and doors
and grows more and more?

I'll Find You

I'll gather you, God, from the blue lupine
and the smoke of the cottage chimney,
I'll collect you from the icefall on the creek, time's pale stiff,
I'll collect you from the beech forest, their gray virgin
bodies that never knew a man,
they keep their hearts up in the branches,
when they get old, they'll put them in a basket
and use them to pay in the shop in the village.
At the end of the village, there's a ruined chapel
with an inscription *Es ist vollbracht*
over the wooden Christ.
I'll collect you from October forests, their leaves burning with a
         question
about you,
from the dark eyes of the Jews who never came back,
all my childhood I ate from their silver knives and forks.
Every moment you hold the world in your hands
so it won't fall.
But it was broken long ago,
it's disconnected, cruel to the bone:
to the chintzy shell of the world.
Pity lives under it.
But I'll set you up, God, in the heavenly spheres,
and the Plain of Truth,
until a demon will remain of you,
or an old blind worm that doesn't care about anything,
I'll surround you with the descending crowd of angels
and a series of hells, from the dead doe on the path and its blind eyes
of eternal sister, my sister,
with a wooden village Christ who governs
this sphere of heavens,
here he's your son.
You left evil
sown in all levels of creation
except yourself.

Every morning I rub the sand out of my eyes.
Every evening a hard dark fin presses my heart.
But I'll cradle you on the silver knives and forks
       of the slain Jews
like a wonderful, perfect boy
         over the pudding with raisins
         on the Plain of Truth,
where icy winds
sough between the Nothingness and the Good,
a man crossed between them, of his own will,
like everywhere.

The Images Emerge from One Point

The images emerge from one point
and line up one after another,
                              like moments.
It is the First Day – the idea of Good
                        or just TO BE –
the land of ideas
is a land of love,
        anywhere.

But they say: No, it's only a Metaphor,
they say: You can't take it
                              so personally.
All the world's terribly personal,
its questionnaire throws
    haunches of memoirs at me
    every morning,
    they devour time like fuel,
    rocket-propelled, that shoots me off.

But somewhere there must be
the homeland of Ideas
like a homeland of love,
where I've been living:
    who haven't harmed anybody,
pure like meadow-saffron, my smile a balloon
kicked up to the heavens,
addressed to all.
A broken creature!
The words from catechisms
stand upright, they're
skittles
you have to go between them,
now they change into the hanged
tugging at your coat
they're your convicts

and take you at your word
you have nothing
you're dumb
have to begin
     again.

III

Between the Icons of Biting Questions

Between the icons of biting questions
and in the uncertainty of gifts
Where to start? Which word
      to choose?
A God?
A Good?
Or just put leg
    before leg
and step out into the abyss of mists –

World rolls its rubbish
before it
and presses the heart like a ball
How to breathe
      the more to speak?

A woman with gold watches
on her hand without fingers
in the Jewish Cemetery in Prague
A boy smearing mandarin slices
on the walls of the hospital corridor –

Why? they asked him. Why, rabbi,
are such crippled children born
who cause no one any harm?
Is it because of sins of the parents?
He answered simply:
God will show His deeds
on them.
But if he doesn't, are we to blame,
caught in the icon of evening,
flowering oleander,
viscous doubt?
Or the fissure goes through all of creation,
through the ranks of angels, the line of the Covenant?

God's creation, though perfect,
must be imperfect, because God can't
create Himself.

Oh logic, poor logic!
The cauldron of the Mediterranean, the cicada can't help singing,
Paradise's garden of olives,
you imitation of God, you idol!
You!
The icon of Yes,
the icon of No,
two children play in the sands of the heavens.

Eggs, Newspaper, and Coffee

Eggs, newspaper, and coffee
are the first lie of the world,
saying that it's
                        in order.

What order, while the whoredoms
of Jezebel, your mother,
and her witchcrafts are many?
said Jehu to King Horam
and shot him
                        between the shoulders.

What order, when every morning
the ark's built up,
and the animals outrun
                one another,
wheedle money, bribe Noah:
        Brother, let me in!
Noah's taken in,
the ark rocks on pity, on grief,
a swift stream, the Okeanos of weeping,
spits it into the pan of eggs
        in the middle of the morning.
How the animals shout! How fried they are!
        The latest news from the ark! Come and get it!
                they squeak from the pan,
and above them, implacable as Jehu, an angel cries:
What order?
The news of your heart
is black as night,
ugly as a Medusa!

On the waves of a compassionate coffee,
Noah sails the ship on
past shop shutters slowly lifting up,
around rambling flowers

that open and close
their shining petals,
and breathe out pity
which papers
            the world

Language Is a Foreign Word

When you hit bottom,
language is bulky and hard, logical
like adrenaline.
Like a foreign word.
In the night, airtight, sealed off by disbelief
        from the bomber squadrons
        of the Lord of the World, Robur the Conqueror,
in the room stuffed to the ceiling
with black deeds
fighting with books,
a lamp shines down, devouring the air.
Who said there's no connection
between language and the world? And then
walled himself up
        with a fence of disconnected seconds and impossibilities,
        with a world sliced like an onion,
        sauteeing in the pan,
        that delicacy of cannibals.

You're a miner in the mine, must
work the empty hours away,
you'll wander a long time, alone,
whipped by the screams of animals and children
kicking you up through the gate,
through the gate of the New Jerusalem.

Where

Far away in the heavens there was a cloud churned
out of white bread and sugar budding, a cloud-fever,
cloud-quinine, oh that fever under the northern sky,
men in fur coats, women in fur coats, almost without
any questions, keep silent

    under

the warm surface of grief that swims in the soup, the soup gets cold,
a frozen soup in the white beard, who's a killer and who's not?
A grief not levelled by a churchyard, not distilled by gravediggers,
soup-grief, impossible to ask

    over

which sky the sun's a child's blue,
to smoke about childhood, Samuel from the next class, a ballet's
hierarchy of heavens, an opera's hierarchy of colours, an apple tree
flowering green with white leaves, don't ask under which sky
people don't die, thrown away

    behind

the cup with coloured glaze the conscience rests,
men go out hunting, MEAT! MEAT! – insidious houses topple
under the ground, there are no returns, men,
we'll free an old story of birth, woman and blood,
under the northern sky men with frozen beards don't kill
women alienated by the children,
there are laws, for God's sake what laws, everything's

    within, within.

We Don't Know the Shape of Feelings

The triangle of hate,
the circle of love,
the square of fate... we don't know
the shape of feelings. But their colours
draw our gestures. Yellow veil of the void
dresses the separation.
And she's red, that woman
with a crown, a false card
thrown away by the children:
who are blue, running
                    in the garden,
looking for the hidden figures of animals.

The world is full of love like a balloon,
and equally vulnerable,
all your lives are slowly
                    spreading out
into the set of coloured cubes,
one fitting to another,
little homuncules inside –
            wide-open orchids,
they grope after anyone they can catch and love.
Day overflows like an ice cream
and the cubes won't fit back together,
it's just one erect moment,
a Hiroshima – or is it Berlin? Thousands
            of pink hawthorn petals
            fall on the corpse
and love inflates the world,
someone's crying –
Hiroshima, hawthorn, dead balloon
and all the time
someone's crying

In the Dark-blue Babylon

Facing the all-white sky
love is but
   a courage.

You won't go back home, won't find
          either a father or a mother,
every door
will lock in front of you,
you'll stay forever in this dark-blue Babylon
because you're a blockhead.
    – No, I'm not!
     I'm not, I have a brave heart!

Time

Time's not a drift but a fall
                    from Yes to No
                    from No to Green –
                    Yes, Time adds
                            pears and apples together!
Time's a falling into
    the heart of the concave Earth
    where the facts, the fat acts
                    of the country
                    resonate, battered by
                    the white bones of humanity.
Time's a falling over
    the edges of the flat Earth
    into the cell of the universe
    where there's not even a buffet
    with pea soup and beer
Time's just an idea
    falling on the sisters,
    venerable, black, closed
        to the cloisters of virtue –
    a pedagogical idea of God
    in the kitchen of eternity
    And you, man of nettles, awake and
                    endure!
Time's a test case, falling into
    the jail of spring, summer, and late falls
    but together with you!
And, as retribution, you'll receive
    the charm of running on green grass
    where all-human vegetables
    and humanitarian fruits grow.
    A pilgrim doesn't want them. He looks for
    scraps of statues
        from the Wheel of Fortune.

He looks for Justice.
For the little finger of Grace.
For the white bones of humanity –
oh, and hopscotches over them
to the centre of the universe
where the Holy Virgin in the buffet
hands out the pictures of saints
and serves pea soup and beer
to the pilgrims and the dearly departed...

The Glass Dead in Old Polska

Yellow star shines like a cancer and pestilence
sewn into the skin and won't
exonerate God.
They gave me pills, and I've got a headache.
I'm talking to a gray cloud, as if it were
God, then
it disappears.
Well okay, the Devil's necessary,
balancing the halves
of the equation,
and in the middle, Nothing,
like someone's death.
So tell me why pain exists?
It ought to vote, break
the balance –
marshal the sun's regiments,
and give meaning
      to the cube of meat,
      the hyperbola of the universe...
Time's treading along one of its sides.
The other's inhabited
      by monsters, stars, and the dead.

     Through the holes between
     crowds of dead Jews
     return home every night
     to have their glass of coffee.
     Every night they sit
     on the glazed verandas
     in a house on the hill,
     gazing at the birch trees
     while the glazed living sleep.

I'm standing on the terrace and shouting:
I have an immortal soul!
Nothing more, not even a tomato-bed
in the anabolic anaconda of the universe,
but two children and an immortal soul!

  – In the spark inflamed by God
    blown up by the Devil,
    blown away by the people,
    the glass dead, a sugar cube
    between their teeth, calmly drink
    chicory all night long.

Ash Death

My death's growing there:
on that hill of ash trees
where I put on
for the first time
my ash wings and flew.
She began to feed on
my blood there. She munched my bones.
While I flew down the hill
        to the beehive,
and then just ran
on the road to the valley,
where the blue forest shone
        like future lives.
Ash death! Wrapped in words
        as if in lard
on that hill of ash trees and forever.
I had her on my
shoulders like a cat.
She grew with me.
She led me like a fake lighthouse
        leading soldiers astray.
But she was mine...
And then a whale of a city
swallowed me, and I was inside, with lamp-posts
and a gang of cops,
checkered by the cafés and their theatre
of jumping wine-dwarves.
I lit the road
with the whale's blubber. She sat
      on my shoulders.
Then she spread out, widening with children
        as with the wandering hands of trees.
And as it was my life, so shall it be
my death, paradisical, implacable,
all the while disputing
the archangel:

showing ten wax masks to anyone
but just one smile for me
       on that hill of ashes,
either a sneer or an honor, just for me
in the last second
behind the wax teeth.

Ferry Livorno-Sardegna

I hear words coming
    bold, lined up
        like brushstrokes
    or like a ship looking for its course
        in the ocean.
The captain believes a hundred meters ahead
the sea's the same as
    a week ago, as yesterday.
The captain believes the sun will rise
and the steward believes tea in the cup
won't turn into coffee.
Or into a woman:
    blonde hair's
    falling on the table, on the hand
    covered with fine hair, on a teaspoon,
    blending into the tea,
the passengers rub
their cabin-window eyes, behind them, inside,
you can see the white spray,
and fish fall from the mouth
        on the jam.

Nothing of this belongs to me
courage whistles in the air
and makes my earrings ring
and makes me believe
    I'll hear it again
I'll go up on deck
  and see in the sky
  an orange
  with a human face
  and a slow smile
    for you and me, captain and steward,
    and all the fishes on the jam.

The Worst Is Awareness

that only I remember the afternoons
at the bus stop, where a dog with a sick eye
looked sadly at my mother –
heat, steel-plated waiting room, blood

And all those afternoons not even I
remember
must be in the minds of angels not yet created
and one day they'll blossom
scattering images of us, light
from the past, the judgment upon the dead,
they'll parcel out
           the heavens.

Gifts

It's only your way, nobody
can help you with it, nobody
is nobody.
Unwittingly, though of good will,
they're bringing you gifts
which you redress, then
give back.

The first is *I*, as seen by others.
The second *I*: how you see yourself.
Another *I*: the way
you'd like to see yourself.
The last *I*, as seen by God.
Oh battles, oh robberies, and cosmetics!
I
like a diamond lit by limelight,
in the window of a jeweller,
how bystanders admire
the changing configuration
of facets!

What suffices the soul?
Where do the demands lead you,
red carpets cast
under your legs
to tread on
soundless like a fossa
to the fizz of champagne
in the middle of a congress.
'We search for the principle
of the soul.'
And small devils
the red hall is postered with
shoot out tongues at us.
What suffices the soul?

Where to turn, from where
does the light shine, what's
inside?
You pull two
children by the hands,
like an old Indian woman.
Alone? What's that?
Everybody's here,
all the time.

All Souls

Genius is
a sowed heart of nature,
a chrysanthemum's mouth
smiling to death from below
    from the sun of the dead,
      the light of the mirror –

Come and buy candles, lemonade
 and candy floss!
 It's All Souls...
The kiosks sit
    by the cemetery.
We buy pink cotton for the dead
and flowers for the tomb of the genius –
For Time's tomb that never
    could tie its shoestrings.
  It's All Souls...
But what of the others? Who never owned
      the world,
just the horribly narrow sector of a circle,
    an eye of the hopscotch figure
they were never able to jump from –
and drank rum and kümmel,
drank the worst gin to the dregs and
    floated up to the angels...
Chrysanthemums in the vases sip
 the yellow lemonade,
  it's All Souls
and I pray to You, God:
Let me go through November again
 to the cemetery kiosks,
hand in hand with mother, because father
isn't here, we're bringing him
flowers and wreath, the heart's antechambers,
which mother will pour out
    before him,

mother, the purler of bad news.
Let me go again through the city
up to the cemetery,
and then the past will become
                              an image
like a town abandoned years ago,
still with the upright hillsides of houses,
and the slides of surging curtains,
but without men –
where all my childhood elves
haul up hidden hoards now
    from below.
Then I'll stand there,
    peeled like a turnip,
    shining like a carrot,
and the story's skull will flutter
    like a rogue hanged on rope
and I, stuck in the eye of the hopscotch figure,
will hear the void in the story's skull
responding to me.

What Is a Man?

What can I know?
What shall I do?
In what may I trust?
    a man asks, thus being himself
    a question.
A question covered by flesh
walks the earth,
smells an acacia,
and gazes at the sea
filled with stiff stone monsters.
What to do now?
Catch time like a fish?
Catch you or me?
Time's a fluid. But what's
the difference between time and me?
Tangibility of eyes, of hands holding
a cup of coffee –
and again, of eyes that can see:
an eye sends its own light
and the sunlight
joins it,
from their kiss
a yellow crowfoot raises its big head.
Genius
is a continuous presence.
Neither WAS nor MEMORY
can enter.
Like God: having
everything before you,
Pacific and Atlantic, a hand
encircled by reproach,
and paddle-steamers on the Mississippi.
Women rolled over by men,
men rolled over by women,
all flat like gingerbread hearts from the fair.

What is a man? asks a man,
What is a man? asks a woman,
surrounded by hermaphrodite slugs
in the Garden of Eden.
And they reply, in the moment,
but their answer's as out of date
as an old cheque.
Doctor, mason, gardener:
each compounded from the set of acts,
how I envy them every afternoon!
But in the morning
the unfinished world
calls out its word – its God –
the crunch of a roll constructs
the Tower of Babylon
and from its oven
Christ falls down,
a small crying mouth,
I'll take him into my arms, and bear him
till evening.

And Still, We're Moving Forwards, Backwards, Left and Right

And why should it end well?
Why suppose I'm better than
anyone who's suffered like a dog –
not better, but worse,
and still
there's a question of
    the suffering & the creating, the man.
God's Providence
spreads its veils
    like spiderwebs.
Without My consent you can't even
shake your head!
             He said,
looking at the clots of murderers
          marching
through the nettles of commands,
through the Protestant Bible's black letters
of total predestination.
How to enter into Liberty?
Which word is mine? The kind,
        or the mocking?
Is it a story, or a prayer?
I'm its composite,
like an insect's eye,
and the world's equally
        multiplied,
a bee defends itself
by stinging the world right back,
wanting to kill. Kill
all of this, even myself
if Hell didn't exist but it does,
and pity and sorrow,
heaven waves its petticoat at us,
and sends calling cards,
today at five the doctor's coming,
get up, wipe the table, make some tea.

Floating Through a Sea of Ice Floes

So shall we be judged
just according to our deeds?
Or our faith
will decide it,
the one we weren't up to,
casting doubt as a shadow,
attacking ourselves, attacking God,
not knowing how and what to pray for,
but always praying –
in the cockcrow,
in the face of mangy hospital cats,
or at home
   in the cruel, cheerless light of morning
when dawn's a cliff
   floating through a sea of flat ice floes
   inscribed:
      Hopelessness Infidelity Violence
                    Booze The End.
Just The End,
no merry before-hells,
no anecdotes on beer.
The End when you float, arms outstretched
in the icy silence of the universe,
and the purring of stars, those cats
you can't hear anymore.

Sister Irony

Sorrow is boring.
How you float through its timelessness –
The square of window is gray and boring.
The globe of sky is gray and boring.
People, two-legged creatures,
walk, back and forth,
injuring one another.
The others watch,
some write it down.
Who started it? Who's guilty?
Sorrow drinks beer. Irony
sips whiskey. She's my sister:
the same as me, but
where I cry she laughs.
She survives everything, immortal
like a protozoon
or grave digger,
flipper of pancakes and tears, a liar!
Being in love, but with whom?
Herself? A laugh?
One day I'll get her drunk,
shake out that restraint
the space between.
Below, I'll see a sea crop up.
A herring in the sea.
And above the herring
there'll be crying
an orphan universe –

Everyday Tablet

Sorrow
only dies from greater sorrow.
It's the way
of the dead:
one leaves room for another.
But sometimes, at night,
they're all here,
leaving
their images in the mirror:
at the entry,
there's mother
putting on my coat, going
to the laundry;
father's caught
in the hall mirror,
a beret on his head,
hands behind his back,
walking around, listening
to the ideas, trying
to understand.

In the bathroom, naked and smooth,
all my past
selves.
How they vaporise in the hot air!
With a trickle of blood
in the corner of my mouth.
All the words are gone.
The roads remained,
like holes etched in the air
under the ceiling:
a tree in the middle
of the fields,
a flat at the quay
cluttered with belongings and books,
my past selves.

They aren't all totally dead,
not yet.
Still, they produce gestures
like instructions for invisible
angels of air
to send them off
in their wicker baskets –
say, to Maryland!

Or to Paris, but simply
far from the rifle barrels
of these days, shouting
rags to rags,
rabbits to rats –
if you put something inside
it'll drop out
compressed
to a box,
a brown, packaged
everyday tablet,
thickened
soup of death.

The Holy Comedy

Not stepping into the entry,
OVERTHROW inscribed above.
I'm not
a creature going to slaughter,
the moments nip at me,
I'll wave my hand
change them to cocktail snacks
to send to you.
There's no road here, only heaven
with the crucifixes and skittles of Madonnas,
it smells like gingerbread,
this kitchen of catholicism,
the pope crushes pepper, no,
it's gunpowder
for the medieval monsters
from the end of the world,
with a face instead of breasts,
one leg
or devil's hoof,
it's them, here
it's me,
oh Vatican!
We're eating fishes, feeding pigeons
in the colonnade of the church,
next to us, in the restaurants,
forks stick smiles
on white tablecloths, it chinks, oh holy
delicatesse! holy fishing!
'Poetry is vain and harmful for God.'
The puckers of my heart spread out
like lungs,
you dropouts, you sweethearts, come in!
Behind the bloody folds
there's a performance going on,
everybody's on stage –
Humility, Wantonness and Lust

barehanded
bareheaded
round and round
wound
and blood.

The Swing in the Middle of Chaos

Sometimes, the dead come. Kinder
than the demons,
they repeat they love us,
scramble a watery goulash,
instant and distant moments.
They say I shouldn't
go over the edge, where
an unfinished world lives, turning to stone
moment by moment.
Where road is a statue of road,
        made of dreams, mustard and tears.
From which pour the cottages of categories,
the short circuit of metaphor, eyes like compasses
        in the tunnel leading to the void,
            words!

A child rocks in the swing
        in the middle of chaos.
Chaos is white, vermiliony gold,
blue like a room with a candle
        in the middle,
        room left by someone dead.
A child rocks in the swing and keeps
her eyes open. After a while, she'll go up
to the kitchen
for a snack.

In the kitchen, there's bread and butter
        with mustard.
Where childhood lives.
It's not me. Someone else
used to go to the fridge
to taste the caviar. Childhood: caterpillar and butterfly,
connected by information –
and it's detail, the Monarch of
        Memory's Empire:

it's the detail that hurts.
Mother, not you, but we
come upon the dead,
turning to stone every moment, changed into
statues of mustard, otherwise
we can't live.

The Moon Soup

(for Jaroslav Seifert)

The moon soup,
opaque yolk on the night sky
salty yellow poetry
I'm living off

there and here, in the room where the poet
lived, walking on crutches,
looking at the red light of the stack.
He saw it's a lighthouse,
put aside crutches, went to bed,
lighthouse pointing to the moon,
of what use was all this, he wondered,
what was it about?
Should I have enjoyed it more, or less?
He can't catch it yet.
So he gets up, sits on the stack and flies
to the moon, tastes the moon soup, from above
everything's clear, like for God,
a man parcelled out like the country filled with fields,
blind alleys, holes, the balks, salt
tickles his palate,
he starts to laugh.

The Epigones of Time

The year is old.
What did I offend? What did I do?
What did I miss?
I ought to ask
like Pythagoras
every evening
Not to eat beans
not to take up what fell down
There's a sun here, and
our only mistake's
the lack of concentration
When I reach a hand out to
yesterday's morning
there's a void
Poets are backward beings
said Nietzsche
a bridge to past epochs
Eternal epigones
say the epigones of time
I, epigone, put words
like eggs in the pan
maybe they'll open
yesterday:
a broken kaleidoscope
of colours, sentences, places
the scrapyard
I'm going through
taking up what fell down
A sort of simplicity,
the focal simplicity of
gesture, world, word
Yes, I say,
that's me.
I'll do it. I'll make it.
Here.

Draft in the Head, Draft in the World

And still, trying to find a changeable synthesis
in a world built of scraps,
discrete, separated
images of a filmstrip.
Oh, those enterprising carcasses in machina mundi!
Oh, that smoke, from the factory of dark pap!
Deep craters of crying!

There's a draft in the head, draft in the world.
'How can you speak of liberty
if you have any memory?'
the man said heading to the pub, 'At the Pork Rib,'
to balance humility and self-love,
let the sands quietly, intangibly
move the dunes in his heart –
there was silence inside,
silence.

There's a draft in the head, in the world
in a mixed day,
confused cocktail
of smells, gestures, words –
'We seek the unconditional
and always find just conditions.'
Compound the puzzle, catch sight of
uncreated light,
through a window of an icon, a window of the other,
catch sight of Jesus.

There's a draft in the head, in the world,
twisted like a question mark
from mash
for the masses –
And you said in the morning,
at the kitchen table:

'If I were a protozoon
I could stand it soon.'

Merciful Madonna,
one distinct line on her face
spread her smile out at the world –
at me:
'So let you go,
        let you go.'

The Moments

The moments turn aside
you stand between them
want to pick one
to enter.
All the instants you've put off,
the reservoir of days, the inflatable balloon
of the past universe
begins behind your head
but when you turn your back
it turns back, too.

Peas and skyscrapers grow
in the interval between the moments.
A dustpan blossoms.
Down in your heart, they say
Christ lives.
Or at least the Holy Ghost.
Oh Holy Trinity of hors d'œuvres, main course,
and dessert!

Behind the moments, an eternity.
Like the plain of the Elbe, but
icy and bright, a frozen
brilliant ocean
of infinity.
Time has broken off,
like a floe,
he's its child
wanting to play,
tossing the seconds about
like skyscrapers,
at you,
you've got to catch them,
beat him off

then fall in
here, inside, where
you live, your own
child, a step
from birth.